First edition
ISBN 0-935992-38-3

Cover art and author photo by Alyssa Matthews
Typesetting by Doormouse

United Artists Books
114 W. 16th Street, 5C
New York, NY 10011

unitedartistsbooks.com
spdbooks.org

# DON'T DRINK POISON

Sarah Anne Wallen

United Artists Books
New York, 2015

## TABLE OF CONTENTS

Do you wanna stay in bed all day?

YEAH!

Do you remember feeling any other way?

NO!

— Le Tigre

## WITH UNDYING CELEBRITY I AWAKE

with undying celebrity I awake
with a mouthful of conscience
I awake with my mouth full
of my dreams and dryness
I need a glass of water

sometimes I just wander
around the streets
because I can't go home
or I won't and so
I go places and sit there

the fun times happen
in a kind of reel
in the movie biz talk
which I know a lot about
babysitter to the stars

which superhero are you?
I like Batman because he's fucked up

with undying trepidation
I proceed with the day ahead
with a mouthful of string cheese
I stole from someone's fridge

hello, dear godly creature
show me the way
I can see no way
out of this was a line
I wrote in a poem

all existence is free-
association, free-
writing, writing
for free

I have an urge
to do it all for free
and then die

## CALL TO ORDER

*for Tony Iantosca*

and despite or in spite of
all the angry fishes feeling
above and not under
the weather, whether or not
the fishes know how
we could call them pissed
take a whiff of goodbye
to the good and plenty lifestyle
form of bills and meds
not drugs, beheadings not hugs
that snail got clean crushed
crisscross apple salsa like
I think they sell that at
Trader Joe's where I throw
a big unreasonable tantrum
regularly for the paparazzi
talking like 'bout a Revlon ad in Elle
and how my Pog is worth more
than your Livejournal archive
and how could I forget
the drama circle with bongos
in the hills of Mecca?

# MOVING ROOFTOP PICTURE SHOW W/BUFFALOS

buffalo rooftop    buffalo seashell
buffalo wings against the image of sunset
great jog of sand pipers    crammed in a box
mother crab    orange dressings
a crab in person    cash crab    a buffalo you pay
bovine legs in the surf    cowgirl undertow
western shehorse    sea cow crab of the coast
set to sink    cloud buffalo    cloud crown
buffalo crowd into me    Curly Sue
buffalo soup the color of horseshoe crab
clap trap    clam song    a wail clapped quiet
shut buffalo boxes    orange on the blue
a light square buffalo building    big craze
big stare into outdoor theater haze

morning!    it's morning    it's night
slow shoes    cool shoes    cool lightning
pearly hues    cool lighting    it's a show
my flight path strayed from as a fire
as a fire boils shellfish in water
witches amid a clump of kelp    blood in a goblet
gobs of it    cups of buffalo    juice of a cub
skin of my fist    blood on my tongue
in my mouth having tasted the witch
potion for love    brew of the sea cow

poem of the trench    portions of moon movement
sleek like buffalo    graze on the vast green grasses
slow breath on a hot mug of buffalo
blonde crabs in a cave
white buffalo hairs on a pillow

remember my name    how I wade
voice of the sea cow buffalo crab
my shell echoes on a cracked horizon
melt of cow tongue clam crayon buffalo landscape
buttered sea leg    I like it on my chin
crabby patty cake    my chin on my gun
pool for cows    I like to see it boil
I like to shoot my gun

moving rooftop picture show with buffalos
a ghost creeping into the shot
movie of my thoughts on this woman
she photographs the space her body leaves
crab-like in her movements
grace of a sea cow or buffalo
outlined by pure buffalo sunlight
the wind taking up loose clothing as wings or fins
big dive into the deep blue sea and sand

by the power of the trench and gyre
salt of boil and blubber    o buffalo rooftop
seeded horizon    all my idols are tragic
all that crab bait    spoiled crab

sand in my drink      in a box with seashells
beneath the bed    planet of sand and metal
rooftops attracting an orange light
golden buffalo brine    brown beer of the crab barrel
ship of sea glass knocked together    who's there
a slow and secret whisper from the trees
meets midway between the sky and sand like lightning
buffalo charge    bright charge of crab

## WHEN NIGHT COMES

when night comes
the source cries out
for death in its dark body
and of it too, sensations
of serpent or ox, or better
yet an otter, a toucan
great connoisseur death is
of shaped flesh and the word
paired with flesh often

the source cries out
for death, the states
at night breathe black
walls of false quiet
even post-mortem
something audible and too
the source's cry straddles
the states, shifts in
concentration happen
with light and water
and so forth the moon tugs

to death, to death marches
the day, it ends at night
and night is not itself
a death so much, although

the source cries out at that
time, arriving here
as a thought and yet
and yet something other
than that alone emerges
or is otherwise in recession

## ANCESTRY.COM

part-time queen
of three countries
twinned redhead
a trimmed name
some neglect
l'shana tova
great homo
her throne drops
on an island
body of ribbons
feminine nestle
caregiver structure
that boat brings
good fortune
flower play
the shtetl's online

## HER BATTLES

impulse to quote
subdued here
what she said
on the line
a damn dirty
fight this is
a celebration
pink fizz
le tigre swings
between vines
the high road
and rather
than pools
now islands

## INSIDE OF IT

I am part of the sky
and the grass outside
I am apart from it
but also part of it
the grass and the sky
and also the trees
maybe I'm more like the trees
reaching up to the sky
my feet planted on the ground
I want to be inside of it
I want the grass and sky inside of me
I am part of the trees
or in part I am the trees
my basil plant needs me to water it
I place it in a sunny spot
I eat the leaves
I am a little basil tree
in a sunny spot
the air feels cool
I breathe it into my lungs
the branches in my lungs
resemble tree branches
part of and apart from everything
the sky and the grass

## BECAUSE YOU LOVED ME

there are birds around
the sounds that birds make
are referred to as 'chirps'
bird calling is a skill that some people have
some people say skill is relative
one can go to a place referred to as 'the catskills'
cats are skilled at catching birds
birds eat worms
the early ones
some words are easier to pronounce than others
some words sound like other words
these words are referred to as 'homonyms'
'homo' is a prefix that means same
'prefix' is a word that refers to the beginning
of a word
mockingbirds imitate the sounds
that other birds make
they lack their own unique chirp
these birds might mock each other
mocking other birds
and eventually themselves
resulting in an endless loop of mocking
the sounds that crickets make
are also referred to as 'chirps'
some modern cars chirp
when they are unlocked remotely

once I hit a bird with my beamer
and the windshield cracked
pigeons are also referred to as 'rockdoves'
doves without the above prefix
are used to symbolize hope or love
doves are also referred to as 'lovebirds'
a term that also refers to a couple of humans
displaying affection

## QUICK RAIN

grey clouds just rolled over heavy
clouds in paintings or poems
may represent breasts
there was a quick rain just now
the grey clouds have become white
clouds may also represent bellies
in poems or paintings
clouds may be said to have bellies
when they are full of rain
when the clouds are grey and heavy
clouds fill and empty as do bellies
not all bellies become full
some people feel guilty
for complaining about their sadness
I am a person who does this
sometimes when I feel sad I eat a lot
sometimes when I feel sad I don't eat at all
it seems to be all or nothing with me
it is easy to wallow when it rains
when the sky is full of grey clouds
my mood is a grey-colored sadness
I feel full and heavy and inclement
tears are not like rain
watching a man cry
is sadder than watching a woman cry
women often say this

men do not like to be called sensitive
it is a feminine quality
I imagine that men are more likely to paint clouds
which are meant to represent breasts
full white breasts that fill a dress as a sky
sometimes when I cry
my tears fall between my breasts
some white clouds look like cotton
clouds look like they would be soft to the touch
but they are just water vapor
breasts are soft to the touch
my breasts are very soft and large
breasts are soft because babies
are meant to put their faces against them
I want to feel my baby's face
against my naked breasts
while it was raining just now I felt like crying
I am white but not like the clouds
sometimes I feel guilty for being sad and white
this is problematic and then I feel guilty
I would like to be more like a cloud
just now it rained and the clouds changed
my change is not so obvious
I am not like the clouds
my breasts are saggy and white

## WATCH YOUR EYES (HERSTORY)

I'm the french fry of your heart
I'm smart
a word to the wives
table-thumping hooligan
tree trunk loogie
watch your eyes
I'm dawn
I'm one big sun of a solar system
a real cunt
fountain of motherlove
full of sounds like
declarative statement
I'm wet stoned
boned structure
maidenform
foreign horn
total corndog
I'm in up-close proximity
I'm a dreamy waterfall
a dream of falling
franco-philistine
rat rat bunny rabbit
duck duck muck
the noose is loose
gimme a boost
I'm tumblr

I'm chemistry
I'm forever in a bottle
red-genie version
twitch-nosed sniveler
I'm all cat
and mousey
dipped in milkshake

## CRAYON CRACKER

*for Pareesa Pourian*

wax on the patio
a square of it soars
above with feeling

she lost
a tooth there
in the high shelf
in it a name
this shape
thrown uphill

or is it a jelly
murmuring
in a lighted
spot?

some illumination
or a skewer
this piece
of cheese

fishy, come find me
a swirl of lavender
clouds of it make
my throat itch

at my suggestion
this golden graham
this burnt toast tossed

a little grit
tooth among
the pebbles

a gate     agave
a window hole
there fleshy

were it a swarm
of colored
worms entwined
I would have
avoided sunlight

royal rays
of emergence
repulsed around

this is a friendship
a noticeable grey swoop
and so much gold
with wool for a cushion

I want to see
a face in this

to remember the tiger
soaked in gas
and a match in mid-air
forever stopped

onion prisms
stuck to the
pan handle
you rest in front
of the TV
with a glass
feeding our cat
our food
I want to be
part of everything

the moon
is the color
of Herman

some nourishment
penetrates this
image     pervades
the space somehow
with allergy attached

the need to discover
something hides
under a moment
recurring at random

## RAINBOWS ARE PROMISES

what if having sex
was like giving birth—
your loved ones all there
holding your shoulders
telling you to breathe

we are inside
of a great big mystery

womanhood
is so interesting

## FEELINGS HAVE RAINBOWS

I like the word spectrum
speculum
speculate
hydrate
menstruate
especially
actually

the feel
of prism
is
um
that my
drink?

## PEOPLE ARE FEELINGS

as time moves
and space
and I move
the couch
closer to
the window
my moves
are timed
to music

## FEELINGS ARE PROMISES

having become a bead
in fantastic daytime
thoughts about threading
beds become beads

in wanting to be a bead
a thread travels through
dreams are a way
the brain can do this

dream thing of want
thought of in real time
the body passes around
a not-blocked bead

## PEOPLE ARE RAINBOWS

you get by
with light
in light of it
in lighght
of it all
the getting by
I mean you
are my eyes
trained on
that horizon
where you arc
a foreground
to a thought
about people
shedding light
not quite
intentionally
full of it
I leave it
at the end
underneath
the natural
order of things
some people
get called birds
smell like tuna

down there
if people
are rainbows
are rainbows
political?

## RAINBOWS HAVE RAINBOWS

like it or
like what
choice is
there even
had ever

have
having have
like half
of have's
usual has
half helping
lack like
this much

what
a choice
light makes
how or not
in light
not how
like that

like this
big if
or yes
butt
out

## UNITED STATES

I.

With green &
purple, red
& blue. &

heaving, each
in places
tacked with

bells on. Struck
the hunger weight
& drag.

Pears shades
a demon yolk.
It goes aglow

& ashes
for a swirl.

II.

Indicative of hairs
of mental bloat.

Syrupy rhizome
tether—overages.

A dot in a dot
& in a dot
a dot. &
next to them.

Inching outer
plains. For sight-
line tokens.

III.

Of windows gurgle
soap notes. All
fresh & clean
& comfy
taps a sill.

Frothy elect
pound reflects
the sun red pink
in blue. Added
to the fore. In

doldrums roundness floated.
Travels
down in

thinking going down.

In green & fresh.

IV.

Paces ocean floor
a foot.

Some doorstep.

A shoving lacking
touching orange.

Hiccup clucks
of past-ness.

Envelopes
a squeaking.

A ring to hum
quick feeling under

softly.

V.

Of swamp propulsion
fringes.

Jacket radar.

Needles—
knives and needles.

Into it
at nine

at season standing.

Shuffles madly
with the crabs

& sea lice feeding.

VI.

One with an open
craw. Tendrils lie in
the wake
& deep.

Of glisten
cough meds
throat lumps
out.

Salt lick dunes
a nightmare, in timing
fiercely.

Breath unto
a frog clump.

VII.

Green &
blue up
there &
there
& there. Too,
a dot, a dot
a jest record.

A host of
clots, a
cancer spasm.

O'clocks in troupes
of sundry routage.

A tree
a bone pump
squabble.

Jump over-easy
fruitcake button.

Bites crooked
mumps a table.

VIII.

Jumbled lakes

a frond monk
hopping.

Mordant boils
open organs

to faces
innards
light.

To swallow whole
clams necked
& little.
Steams

a ghost mouth
wide.

IX.

& over
shoves a tube. Mills
running the drain.
Perfume ado
sprung cut of
drum wax settled
hard & round.
Hitting harder. Cracks
in showers through.

X.

Invade how
tongue, how
umber shocks
a dog. Half-
tweezer buzz
inside of cartridge.

Ceiling sag &
burst. Is a swing

is a bum dance
broken.

With squishy
pillows, hundred
dozen.

XI.

Green to
blue further down
& yet. On

feather bead bed
wind is dirty.

In a bend.

Of slips grind
potion leaves.

In concrete sweeps
of furry insides.

Waves the leaves
create.

Hag in dove corn

sprawl entrenchment.

Purple to red above
for light.

XII.

We
speaks eagerly
& fresh.

Puffy &
leaking
fills a crooked
spot.

To ponder
aim
a yonder
golf.

An ego worth-
while perhaps

if happens
ever is. A

habit

bit of
color.

As needed
dash a cord
worthwhile.

A towel forgot
a note
a dot, a dot
inside. Incensed

libation wend-in
deeps a mold.

XIII.

In the grey frames
fumes the white.

All in a black box
in a red one
lighted.

Horse
in back

eyelet staid

is stiff.

Arm moles
ulcerate

in foam.
& next

to that.

## FREE WILLY

I love myself
when I think
about the whales
because I can't
imagine actually
being a whale
but I can imagine
freeing the whales
from Sea World
in the night
I want everyone
to help me
emancipate the whales
they are smarter
than we are
the cruelty of it
they understand
better than we do
I love the whales
as I love you
and I love life
as long as I can think
I can make it better
for someone else
somewhale else
and that's for real

and even though
I have troubles
of my own
I think they might
disappear if
I could save
even just
one whale

## WE CAN'T STOP

we won't stop
on repeat

I like this song
why?

why do I like it?

you know
the guy
from Grizzly Man
died on my birthday

it's my mouth
I can say
I'm not ashamed

in your face
it's called truth
will you marry it?

it's never quite
what you think

I know
what's going
to happen

a distraction

beautiful H2O

# BRUNCH MONSTER

as for cookies
a cookie within
a cookie
a spicy cookie

the wind talks
a cookie wind
to the moon
if moon was cookie

too many times
a cookie
a spicy personality
a celebratory nugget

interpreting meat
cakes, savory pies
cookie cookie meat love
like duck duck duck duck

the goose is wild
ginger snaps
down a hall
'n oats in a bowl

## EVERYTHING WENT WRONG AGAIN

It's all the same logistical nightmare
with the manicure situation at the moment
and I swear the sun is like
totally a great ball of fire just like
mother always forgot I never would be
and as for the hang-up regarding
the unpaid everything bill
I won't hang up
I'll just never answer

everything went wrong
on the same fucking day
that is "it" as in
"life" meaning "time"
is just an abstraction
the man is just trying
to mind-fuck you
out of doing what feels
good to you to do

I've done it again
this glass of water
is a glass of water
is a glass of water
a glass of water?
if a woodchuck

could chuck wood
what's love got to do
got to do with it?

# A WHOLE SYSTEM

in terms of the regard for the thing about
private time all alone in the almost forgot
what was happening over the duration
of the moment wherein existence happened
or has continued happening since for also
having been brought to the attention
of the first one in mentioning an inkling
about a thing happening for some time
without regard for other times as it was
brought to the attention of the existent
beings which occupy the space who have
thought about thinking of the space occupied
by those who call themselves us who are not
we as in I and you are not themselves with
modality for the price of what's worth it
as giving dictates with the relative sphere
emotions and dreams which contribute
to the thought in the head or the other
who ponders where have I gotten myself
which is a real abstraction happening
in real time to the extent that it can or
the other side of that argument which is null
and void in terms of thinking from another
angle as not a sphere out there is angular
in the shrillest sense of the representation
of a whole system of thoughts which are

dictated by a space or a sphere to a person
or people or us or the construction of you
or me or anybody who can call themselves
somebody and not be some kind of animal
which can't speak except in the atmosphere
of our dreams or some fake construction
of a stilted but familiar world

## BOWL CUT

the smut everyone is reading
is really pretty entertaining
the best parties are when there's
a dance floor in the living room
and I would be lying if I said
I didn't enjoy looking at
the headlines on the trash mags
in line at the grocery store
and everyone knows the song
as death machines roar down
the block, I think my thoughts
but it's just, like, we can't help it
there is a kind of society-induced
drug we get addicted to
probably a chemical is released
when we hear a really juicy detail
I imagine myself in another place
not doing this and it seems totally
impossible because it is
because I'm here and not
doing anything else

## THE HOOK

*for Erika Layman*

have to fight
have to crow
have to go
over there where
the wheat fields
blaze in summer
eggbeaters
while the watchman
gets his wife
re-dressed

on the regular
seed it's been
a scene out of
Twilight time
with the finches
and Saturday
stole the joke
by no fair trend
as maids in summer
kites wend down

at the meeting
we must dream
we must collude

canoodle
we must go
braless as dogs
yes the poodle
by the holy
snort wields
saucers officially
duh of the wrong tint

imperative move
is a wanted charge
virtual hurt
tinge of a frown
in clothes for
having had need
for a coke
or a doodle
with dew about
a windshield

gotta get a visa
gotta have a drink
gotta new lease
for meaning well
take the blue pill
toast to the near
future and may all
your doses be wild

## ENDEARING ONESELF

as it happened it was totally grand
as my piano—as it used to be
but is no longer which holds significance
in the mean time of the world turning

grandiosity is part of the way I speak
and I am but a shadow of my
formal overalls in the part of
the country where that happens

an obvious nod to a tote bag
containing the real coins of this mote
work tucked away in a trunk as good
as it could get itself imagined

or no like got a bae or naw like the kids
say or like the kid in the Kix commercial
says or was it Chex but it was like hey
that child likes it like really likes it

# I GOT A MANATEE FOR MY BIRTHDAY AT THE CENTER FOR BALL PITS

you can say
that's about it
can't you?
how do you
doodle?

have a happy Thursday
pocket my firework
we love them
pool jets
let's go get it

the Indian asked
out your mom
and she actually
said she would go

that knocks me out!

a dime a day
for every whistle
the more the tree
bears fruit, the more
frivolity is worth a damn

those dirty apples

those damn dirty
appurtenances
the locker with
my message is
like the heart
or something
you can say it's like the sun
grows honey from mushrooms
and that this dog
unlike that one from before
has something noticeable
about it

I'll show you the way
on the way
in and of the past
progressive
futuristic iteration
of the language
we speak here

except for
last night I heard
more people speak Spanish
than English and thought
where am I
Mexico?

## INTERNET TELEVISION

I can't help it
Catfish
the TV show

the fish
sucking it all in
with its skin

they sink
you know
instead
of swim

mom called me
her little clam

the TV show

heavy shit
take a hit
of this spliff

yo

there's like
this element

of guilt I have

element
is a good word

a good
table

periodic
at best

hey
hay is for horses

## PSYCH STUDY

as you are
vocalized
forget it

keep it up

a pear
a peach
a leech
freaky deaky

always
should have gone
to that
psych study

always always
I make
a problem
and shape it

I creates it
make stuffs
promises
stuffs like that

an apple
a banana
pomegranate
ya goddamn fruit

a memory
I resist
as it comes

the clouds
I can think about

pigs
you swine

the ever-present
sense of impending
second-coming
which is also
doom I guess

other fruits
goddamn cherries
ape-ricots
folding bone

I likes my tools
if I were a guy
a tool I'd be

come on
come on

come on
to me
the right person
I could fall
in love with you

lemons
lemongrass
wheatgrass shot
smoothie shop
crass suburbia
the grass
I should have
sat on

I could
buy a whole fish
or a lobster

I broke my leg
it aches
where it broke
it just broke
like all
of a sudden

a shudder
a shutter
beating
            in the window-frames of my dream with
the house being ripped apart by a storm while I
submerge myself in the ocean and float off in my
cowboy tuxedo amid the angry waves beyond the
cattail-dotted dunes

## GRUNGE

here there is no coffee
no coffee for anyone

the sounds the birds make
feel like I'm a fish

as a kid I had a teeter-totter
and a tonsillectomy

lah dee dah
a baby's laughter

amid the wreckage
of kindle fire revolution

it burns, it burns
and I want

a chicken nugget
or my own radio show

## WHERE THE CAT IS

finding necessary referent
lacking here a gold stud
dead water elf strokes fins
lobs a root bound for that
loba blackout pause
her migraine cavity holy
feline aloofness only
as a stout stag struts soft
bellies over a salt bake
juice of a lemony flavor
plants the ginger barley soup
soapy tongued malleable fist
with the buds first in parts
internalized stronger rubber
eased epidurally out
scornful not of the dead
mega zombie wardrobe
one of a licked litter
wet disinterested smoker that
mother must be somewhere
having had a genuine jostle
genius form of empathy
what is wrong with me
homely prickled mutt
discovered in a chute
tickled a word for you

a pickle half-done outside
a pigeon nod forward
she likes how it moves
you have a tinted window
glasses hold the bright sun
California here we come right
back where I went all the way
the baby left atop some rice
and a car with many bags
one might have a memory
bucket out the cat already
an amygdala study
reveals an almond
composed of altruism
a leveled eye counted
a family of voles raised
in Eden made due without
psychoanalytic cheek
just fun words to say
bullshit stances sex-driven
pop the soft parts ooze
another's exposed squid feeling
before as a former wanting
classy drone at lunchtime
with a singular eyelid pout
upended put-putting truck
awaits a whole glorious heaven
holy heck a twin's missing
his tooth clouds a mouth

desert storms all amok
into major weed blazing
med munches at bedtime
mirrored closet look
nine climbed in a dress
shoes a dove needled blind
is anywhere again with touch
her heap big hoary crack
clenched in lack of sleep
sincere absence of sweets
Swedish Fish for the kids
quilt light available tonight
read for a boat like
before light illuminates
a gap still attack denied
goodbye my shy old lover
mean model freak passing
out tames her zodiac math
graphs like that mediate
a crunching motion gets it out
her shame her teenage change
jingle-jangles as a crutch
post-Hanukkah posture
kite high in the fig tree
pinning holes in the wall
she calls from an opened thought
my projector works so great
my spirit rooster grows as a lung
as a prism nails Beethoven verve

a promising rainbow
raptor version of a thumb
make that floor thrum psychically
pulp blended lines a screen
people are just happy accidents
I was just accidentally happy
neighborhood trash inverted
prayer hands hang backwards
the cauldron fire is lit
a bag spat spittle as it does
as an onion lady high
on after basil sunlight
mottled color of the cat
cuddled thing molded as hoe
bad handle sad salamander
rocks rounded mineral gatherers
turn to a kid slip palming
boiled koi a double shot
through a hoarse vote
utter nay maker
meet at met in ten
that hen's heart beats hearty
it's all the beets she eats
home repeated thrice
a Jew's advice rejected
for a bad blob of breathing
bugs all over lousy headed
mother super foil covered
hairdo eaten apple season

canine fang in townie slang
ancient hardy sabers
brand name dogtooth
sort of as the saying goes
her depth in toed wort
in sorted jars astringent
of hazel those rolled eyes
that tiny head of yours
a baby on your shoulders
my booze cask filled
why pinken this cheap cheer
the cherry flavor craved
mourning a babe in a cave
in a tin pan alligator pit
gathered sticks consumed
in a fire bowl of dust
unworthy to commune in
perhaps a clucking sound
a bark-like facial structure
nipples have a purpose
swaddle that howling
creature I want
to close out yes
confront the sigh
with a signature
over onus opus
pussy opal abalone
shell for my body
this neckline frames

pretty hairs in a V
clear and beautiful neck
skin a live rotting broad
clear want for destruction
drills a swimmer in too deep
larval state of movement
a mouse imbibes the lead
and sleeps in my hands
youngsters ring the eye gum
le poisson pressed here
just so over clothing
her fort knockers house
a call hath awoken
an open display of feathers
indulge in ornamentation
inheritance of hats or tassels
a lengthy train ride to Philly
finding brussels as a food
is a place we can be
tiny dumplings both ways
nodding kitchen-bound

## THEY'RE ABOUT TO FLY EVERYWHERE

doubt me not
you squirmy devil
I'll be your white girl
for the day and do
your laundry

can I have a beer?
dear butterfly here
have a hummingbird
I want to travel far away
I want to have already
grown up and died

could you eyeball
a noose knot?
how about out
of long-leafed ferns?

I'll lie on the floor
embarrassed—torn
I'd like to dance
release that devil
whatever baby
gimme some tequila

I may not be so
in the loop but I know

Vidal Sassoon
makes my leg
hair silky

## COOLIO

I want to be ready
when you arrive
and look like I haven't
been waiting
long

## COME MY LADY

You make me go crazy
come and dance with me
Killing in the name of
fools on parade
cut the cord
with a pocket full of shells
and the party is jumpin'
it's 11:30
You're turning heads tonight
bounce twist
American Kids come
give me a kiss
I don't want to miss a thing
pardon me I guess
it comes with
the territory
mindless games
I'll never be
the same
I've had enough
and sometimes
I choose water
Release me now
I taste it and breathe
I thought I was everything
what was everything?

Tattooed everything
in sunlight
Cool kids never have the time
jump across the naked
and the void
we don't even care
and down below
never knew the rules
I guess
there's no one around
getting jiggy with it
I know you know
bag with a lot of stuff in it
watch your step
you might fall
don't be silly
You brought nothing real
and I can't take this
set me free     show me the way
Every time you let me down
my time has come
let me     out
say          my name
Every other word
is a hum
tell the truth
something's going down
can you say that?
When no one is around

say I love you
here I am
let me light
your candle
take my hand        don't be afraid
I've got some more in the store
the prayin' just ain't
helpin' enough
you're moving too fast
you don't hear me        come on
come on
what a shame
believe in yourself
right about now
Check it out now        even my mama
thinks my mind is gone
saying prayers
in a tin in my hand
I'm living life
why are we
so blind?
We keep spreading
money and the power
no one's here to teach me
the words we heard
I still see
I'm not dead
All I want to do is have fun
before I die

I'm not the only one
I like a good beer buzz early
in the morning
all I want to do
over Santa Monica
play on play out
still playing the flavor
I can't get it out of my mind
I want to get in
bag it up
Catching feelings
I like the way
you're blowing my mind
that's just me
I'm as real as can be
come on
in full effect
yeah
play on
because I like it
devotion feeling emotion
Don't be afraid to weep
look into your heart
return to yourself
oh hi hi hi to yourself
The return to innocence
oh hi
I'm like a bird
but it's not for sure

thought my love is true
I don't know where my home is
it pains me so much
you don't know me that way
though my love
I want to fly away
every time
every single day
but my love is great
I'm just scared
All I need to know is
a lot less
you should get an extra one
tonight if that's alright
my my my
oh my lord
I'm known can't touch this
I told you school's in
you know
go with the flow
move slide
Stop every time you see
oh yeah
You turn your back
and they're gone so fast
can you tell me
take the time
to find you?
Keep playing

it's a secret no one knows
take your time you say you can
but you don't know
You know you can but you don't
take your time to find you
you say you can
we're still saying please
one last step
give it to me now
When the night has fallen
your dream is breaking
don't give up
The world could fall apart
one dance left
don't let go
What's better?
We'll kick your asses
you're busy
that wasn't very satisfying
what are we living for?
Another mindless crime behind
the curtain
the show must go on
whatever happens
I guess I'm learning
inside the dark
Inside my heart is breaking
fairy tales of yesterday
will grow but never die

I face it with a grin
I love a kill    go on
if you    just go ahead and go
That's what I said now
if you'd just
like to talk for hours
go ahead now
if you'd just
like to talk for hours
go ahead now
come on
Believe
after love
after love
I can't break through
it takes time to believe it
I can feel something inside me say
what am I supposed to do?
There's no turning back
I need love to feel strong
I know that I'll get through this
I don't need you
let's go start a fire
Later on    strike a pose
ain't life a mystery?
I can't explain it
everything I want
I really need
in disguises no one knows

The sky looks dead
cold and damp too long
Heaven send hell away
drown my fear
can I kick it?
Yes of course
wipe your feet really good
yes you can go on then
feel free

## JODIE FOSTER

hi private time
I kiss you

show me the hot spot
have a nice contact
where did you go?

honeypotboiler
bring the guac

they grow up fast
on television
we're gonna need
a bigger book

pride and shame
are the extremes
of the same
emotional reality

scootch over
I'm thinking
it's time to be
really cereal and
let the clock melt

buzzards circle
the buffalos
the cat is in
the closet closest
to the way out

we used to be
beautiful
the front steps
are an escalator
leading to
a beach chair
and people
we know well

I'm having a pickle
and a coffee
it used to be difficult
but now I just eat it

## SAID THE IDIOT TO THE TRUTH

we're not cross-country skiing
a fond thought is not a promise
I am not a cat the future is
an abstraction the sweatshirt
smells like garlic the chard
we grew tasted like dirt bedbugs
are a thing here sentences are
an intuitive understanding of
what's next the world is a vampire
I am not a robot snails fizz and die
when you pour salt on them shoes
with heels make sounds like
an adult is approaching some
succulents look like Mentos
the flue must be open or the room
will fill with smoke Chubby Bunny
produces marshmallow drool
she says a lot of crap but it sounds
great honesty can get you into
real trouble pop songs are often
repetitive she took off her clothes
and wandered through Central Park
one of these things is just like
something else the sky got dark
today it's easy to reconcile buying
new things when you feel like
you've earned it it's patting yourself

on the back being honest all the
time when it snows the sky turns
orange I was kind of thinking a lot
about birds it makes sense that
the world doesn't make sense you
have an angle at which you see
things God is too much about
payback these kinds of things
are distressing muscles are a way
to talk about the beginning crows
flying over can signify a number
of things you can't put in fried rice
like corn pass to the left there is
distilled action in the noun if you
stink at least you leave a smell you
can have a problematic emotion
and make it political being so
dogmatic is usually very suspect
and profoundly embarrassing
experience becomes impossible
and yet is this complete little
shape in your mind we go outside
and things happen to us I don't
succumb to labels or directly
answer questions that offend me
there are living things in the roots
of your eyelashes the internet
is virtual reality pressure change
makes the wind ambiguity makes
some people uncomfortable

## SHOPPING

and that which
chooses you
you also choose

philosophy
religion
cereal
cheaper in a bag
from the bottom shelf

but what best fits
your cupboard
holder of the bowl?

what adequately
challenges but
does not defeat?

## PARDON?

What's that?
I'm translating French to German
and I can't hear you

let's be together always
okay?

that person who loves me
in the future
will buy me a crossword
I mean the Times
every single day

every fucking
knuckle-sucking
day

What's that?
I'm teaching myself nuclear physics
you'll have to speak up

let's be wild and free
'til the end of days

you know, this persona
I make of myself

moving into the realm
of the future says
existence is futile

What's that?
I've said the most profound thing
a person could possibly say?

this is reality

peanut
cashew
it's nuts
these nuts
could totally kill Dan dead!

too bad for that person

little peanut
little squash
little clam
bananagram

you are my sunshine
my only indulgence
you make me grouchy
when you wake me up

## WHY THAT NEXT THOUGHT?

can you pay the rent next month?
better light a candle

have a good time at sleepaway camp
I live to love you forever

I'm thinking of that one scene
he held her arm
in a tender manner—
like my coffee mug?

let us sing
the question song
what to do
oh, what to do
when things
go wrong?

I'm staying home from work
to pay the bills

why that
next thought?

the space gives me room
to think for a second

why bother?

you bother me

swan

## INANIMATE

mirror mirror
I am the fairest
being a Libra and all
my decisions lack error
in that I make none

## ALL IN PLACE

once I choked on a hot dog
once I choked on a big hard
jawbreaker
I accidentally inhaled
a red hot

I desire accuracy
I desire a chord
a choir
to sing my entry
into the stars
the sun

I don't want to burn
I wake up for real

this is the new dream
starring John Cusack
I dine with Dahmer
it's all in his head
Kurt Cobain sings
we all huff glue

here we are
I want to go back

we're under a tree
it's nice here
the grass is cool
little dewdrops fall
to the tips of our noses
the birds sing sweetly
in the branches
overhead

no sex
no king

let's play I'm a hyena
with the voice of Whoopi
walking down the street
nodding to my peeps
and everyone has leprosy

I mean telepathy

I mean leopard spots

## SMOKIN' GROOVES

all over again
red to black and back
again I sing to myself

and that red sweater
that sweaty upper lip
them bit down bloody nails

stroke the neck
wash the cat
fight the power

my picture is called
Time is an Abstraction
I made it last August

that rad electro-punk
in my dreams
my little naked knee

make the bet
ash the cig
eat the filter

## EVENING CONSTITUTIONAL

sun, do not get so
dark and low

it doesn't do
to make a big deal

each day is
another thing entirely

being alive
is hard

I think about
losing my eyes

people decide
to do things

the leaves are turning yellow
the weather is changing, yes

the world is full
of people

a woman jogs
a child screams

it's a happy scream
we're all alright

I desire a crossword
to do

## IT IS TUESDAY

thusly I speak
in the style of Ariana

in response to Alice Notley
responding to Vallejo

responded to by Thurston Moore
whose name begins like a Thursday

thusly I speak
A Thousand Leaves in the car

yellow in my imagination
the city dissolves into itself

driving is knowing another language

little violets dab the landscape
a sunset paints the horizon gold

the language of my driving makes it blur
my culture drives over the grasses

I am a delusional hero
Don Quixote with a ponytail

I speak words with my tongue
I cut off a man's ponytail

and tape it to my head

I am older than Virginia Woolf
older than Quixote

they aren't dead yet
and I'm not

sometimes I think in Spanish
sometimes I dream in red

the Golden Gate Bridge
is my yellow brick road

I sit on my high white horse
hot in the California sun

I stand on this grand old hill and weep
I have very high expectations

I am a hero with a broken leg
I limp along my horizon

thusly I speak
I speak softly

you must lean in to hear me

I cut off your ponytail
and tape it to my head

these are the arms of mercy
her tongue is in my mouth

her mouse has my tongue
the cat got it

Virginia Woolf is the cat with the mouse
in my mouth on the tongue

I am writing a manifesto
a memoir

Ariana watch me walk
your glasses make the sun swell

I speak words with my mouth
my fingers poke words out

thusly I speak

I cut out my tongue
and sew it back in upside down

Emily is in my mouth Bernadette
Mayer is in my mouth buddy

I have my mouth and tongue to pass around
thusly my mouth leaks gems

I speak in long sentences

Woolf is a gem Ariana
Plath is a gem Alice Notley

my mouth
I am not somebody's husband

my foot is in my mouth
I have words in my thoughts

I speak the words in my thoughts with my mouth
there are gems in my pen in my fingers

my iPhone is in your mouth Dottie Lasky
your Adderall is in my ponytail Dana

thusly I speak
I stand among gems

I speak in long sentences
which command a bored attention

and nothing is happening

thusly I love
the long wheatgrasses swept in beach wind

I love Tony and Dan
Lewis and Jamey

Michael and Leo
Pareesa and Zach

Alyssa and Lisa Rogal
gems fall from her mouth

there is a museum of gems
fallen from Lisa's mouth

there are gems on the ground

thusly I love
I decided on speaking love thusly

boldly and with heavy sentiment

if I am to go now
remember my name and my tongue

I speak words I wrote down
softly and at length

as Woolf is in my mouth
a state of mind

if I am to let go
let me enter Thursdays which are Tuesdays now

with a sense of having spoken
gems which must be cleaned and carved

gems just look like rocks at first
rocks fall from my tongue to the head of the cat

where it is on a Tuesday experiencing time
in a linear fashion

writing my biography

## AND THEN

this little path home
was kind of made
of wood and such

the grass was green
and then light brown
and then grey

it all splinters away
in the storm
I dream of often

where I float off
with it and then
under and don't care

## EPILOGUE (MANKIND)

the source cries out for death
I die and my breath abates
my skin grows very cold
and my heart stops dead
the source cries out

what have I done?
and what I have done
is over and done with
dead and done and over
death marches on home

my death is the source
of cold skin and my heart
worn in a frame resembling me
a thing the source-wind blows about

I was always saying
something like that

## ACKNOWLEDGEMENTS

Work from DON'T DRINK POISON has previously appeared in *6x6, The Brooklyn Rail, The Portable Boog Reader 8, Sun's Skeleton* and *Brooklyn Paramount*—deep thanks to the editors. Thank you to Alyssa Matthews for the beautiful cover, and to Marcella Durand and Karen Weiser for the insightful blurbs. Additional thanks are due to Kelsey Bryan-Zwick and Madison Kane Carroll for their valuable feedback and support. This book would not exist without Lewis Warsh, Lisa Rogal, Daniel Owen and Tony Iantosca—"thank you" doesn't seem to cut it, but thank you anyway, and I love you.

Sarah Anne Wallen was born in Manhattan, raised (mostly) in southern California and now lives in Brooklyn, New York. She has two degrees in creative writing—a bachelor's from UC Santa Cruz and an MFA from Long Island University, Brooklyn. In addition to writing poetry and experimental prose, she makes hand-bound, limited edition books as Third Floor Apartment Press. DON'T DRINK POISON is her first full-length book of poetry.